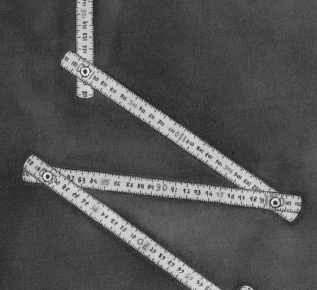

Written by Brigitte Gandiol-Coppin
Illustrated by Eric Provoost

Specialist adviser:
Martin Samuels, B.Sc., M.I.Biol, Head of Science,
Wallingford School, Oxfordshire

ISBN 1 85103 113 8
First published 1991 in the United Kingdom
by Moonlight Publishing Ltd,
36 Stratford Road, London W8
Translated by Sarah Matthews

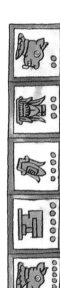

POCKET • WORLDS

Measuring the World

Why do we have to measure things?

In Egypt, fields were measured out using ropes 12 cubits long: a cubit was the distance from a man's fingertips to his elbow.

Desert peoples measured the distance between wells in terms of how far away you could hear a shout or shoot an arrow.

The foot is a very common unit of measurement – although not many people have feet twelve inches long!

When a cat jumps on to a wall, it doesn't stop to measure the distance with a ruler – it works it out instinctively, in the same way that you work out instinctively how far to throw a ball when you are playing. But if you are telling someone how to reach a place, you need to be able to give them an accurate idea of distance, or if you are selling a fish, you need to be able to say roughly how much it weighs. You have to decide on units of measurement that you and other people can agree about and share. **The earliest units of measurement were based on arms, hands and feet.**

The Romans and the Egyptians both used the palm of the hand as a unit of measurement: one palm measured about 7.5 cm.

Feet were used to work out the distance between furrows, paces the distance round a field. But people's feet and people's paces come in different shapes and sizes, and there was an awful lot of variation in very early measurements!

For the Greeks, the amphora was the unit of measurement for honey, oil, wine and other liquids.

In order to make trade easier, and to make it simpler to collect taxes, kings in ancient times arranged that the traders and farmers in their kingdoms all used the same measurements: standard measurements. **Standard measurements gave a fixed value to the length of a foot or a cubit.** But the standards were often only valid within a particular region, and different nations measured things differently – as they still do today!

About 4,000 years ago, Egyptian peasants measured the harvest using a kind of barrel called a bushel; the measured grain was tipped into baskets and stored.

It was important that all measuring instruments could be checked against a standard unit. These standards had to be kept in safe places where they could not be tampered with. In Egypt, for instance, the standard of the Sacred Cubit was engraved on a column where all other cubits could be measured against it. Much later, all over Europe, inspectors of weights and measures travelled with a set of standards in their bags, to check that all was accurate and correct.

In medieval markets, stone containers which could not be moved ensured a standard measure of grain.

Scientists invented special instruments to calculate distance, using the known mathematical laws of triangles.

The metric system

In 1789, the French Revolution set a lot of French people thinking about justice and fairness. It upset them that standards of measurement had been falsified over the years, so that people were easily cheated.

The meridians are imaginary lines which circle the Earth from the North Pole to the South Pole.

They decided to find a measurement which could not be altered, a measurement based on the Earth itself. They divided the length of the meridian by forty million and, after seven years of calculations, came up with the standard metre! **The metre is the basis of the international metric system**, in which measurements are calculated by dividing or multiplying the metre by 10.

One metre = ten decimetres = one hundred centimetres

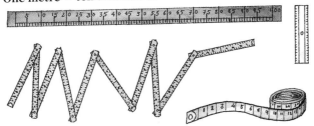

The metric system simplified all sorts of measurements.

Along the straight roads of the Roman Empire, centuries before, stones had been set up every mile, or thousand paces, stating how far it was to the next town or fortress.

Ancient Egyptian ruler

From the Middle Ages onwards, though, travellers had usually calculated long journeys in terms of the days it would take them by foot or on horseback, since they did not know how to use other units of measurement for long distances.

Material was measured using a yardstick, but the yardstick itself could measure anything from 59 cm to 1.39 m, depending on where you came from!

The time taken to do something, whether to travel a certain distance or to plough a particular field, was often the most reliable measurement available. **Nowadays, the metric system has become the accepted method of measurement almost everywhere in the world.** In some Anglo-Saxon countries, though, people use the Imperial system, measuring distances in miles, length in feet and inches, weight in pounds and ounces, and liquids in pints and gallons. In Britain, children in schools are usually taught both systems.

How much do you weigh?
When you measure weight, you are really measuring mass. Weight changes according to the gravitational pull of the Earth; for example, in water and high up in the atmosphere things weigh less, although their mass never changes.

Since ancient times, weight has been measured using scales. The first scales had a long arm, supported in the centre, with a dish at either end; one dish contained weights, the other the object to be weighed. When both dishes hung evenly, you had got the right weight. Nowadays we weigh things on all sorts of different scales.

A weighbridge is used to weigh vehicles and their tonnage.
A kilogramme = the weight of a litre of pure water at 0°C
A tonne = a thousand kilogrammes

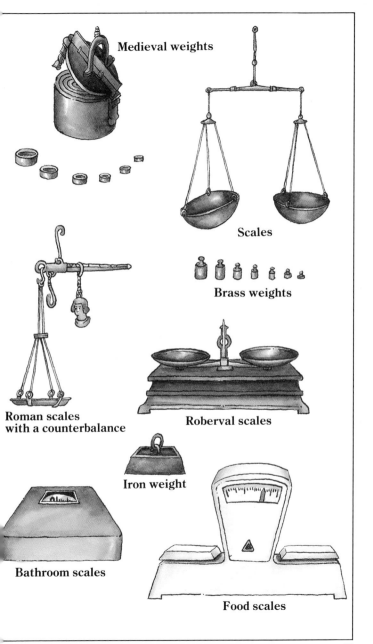

Medieval weights

Scales

Brass weights

Roman scales
with a counterbalance

Roberval scales

Iron weight

Bathroom scales

Food scales

In a market, you can buy things in all sorts of different ways: by the unit, by the handful, by the box or the jar, by the crate or the sackful.

Many cooks use measuring jugs to measure out ingredients. These old ones are made of pewter.

In some countries beer and milk are sold by the litre, in others by the pint.

A pint equals 0.568 litres.

Some things you buy by weight, others by volume. Fruit, for instance, you buy by the pound or the kilo; milk by the pint or the litre.

A litre is the amount of liquid contained in a cube measuring ten centimetres on each side.

In the Middle Ages, most things were sold by volume rather than weight. A merchant could cheat by not filling up the containers properly.

Wood is sold fastened together in blocks measuring a cubic metre.

Aztec calendar

Measuring time

When going to school, or trying to catch a train, you check the time on a watch or clock. But there were not always clocks and watches. Before they were invented, people measured time by the passing of the seasons, and by the rising and setting of the sun.

By observing the way the stars and moon moved across the night sky, astronomers in ancient times calculated that the day could be divided into twelve hours, and the year into three hundred and sixty days. Nowadays, we divide the day into twenty-four hours, the time it takes for the Earth to turn completely round on its axis. We now know that the Earth makes a full circuit round the sun every three hundred and sixty-five days and six hours. It is to make up those extra six hours into one full day that we have three hundred and sixty-six days every fourth, or leap, year.

◀ An eighteenth-century astronomical observatory built in Jaipur, in India

Telling the passing hours

People in the ancient world used to tell the time of day by looking at a sun-dial. They also had other devices such as sand-timers and water-clocks. The first mechanical clocks were invented in the Middle Ages; the regular swinging of a weight at the end of a pendulum turned the hands. Later, the pendulum was replaced by a spring which slowly unwound. When you wind a watch or a clock, you are winding the spring up again. Quartz clocks and watches use an electric battery which sets a quartz crystal vibrating. They are more precise than spring timepieces. The most accurate of all, though, are atomic clocks. They only lose one second every 3,000 centuries! The standard for the second is set by an atomic clock.

60 seconds = one minute
60 minutes = one hour

An astronomical clock shows the movement of the planets.

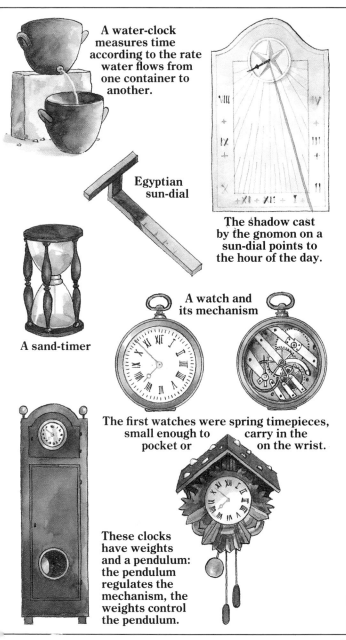

A water-clock measures time according to the rate water flows from one container to another.

Egyptian sun-dial

The shadow cast by the gnomon on a sun-dial points to the hour of the day.

A sand-timer

A watch and its mechanism

The first watches were spring timepieces, small enough to carry in the pocket or on the wrist.

These clocks have weights and a pendulum: the pendulum regulates the mechanism, the weights control the pendulum.

Measuring sound

Sound is the way in which our ears interpret vibrations of the airwaves. Different sounds vibrate at different frequencies, which are measured in hertz. The faster the vibrations, the higher the frequency and the higher the sound.

Keeping time

Music is sound and silence organized together to make patterns. The frequency of the notes which are played, and the rhythm, or beat, they are played in, are very important. When a whole group of people play together in an orchestra, they keep in time by watching the movements of the conductor's baton.

Different notes last different lengths of time – when they are written down, their colour and shape tell a musician how long they should last, while their position on the lines, or stave, shows how high or low the note should be.

There are sounds which our ears are unable to hear. Human ears cannot pick up sounds at more than twenty thousand hertz, or less than twenty hertz. The intensity of sound is measured in decibels. At over one hundred and forty decibels, sound can really hurt.

A metronome provides the beat for a musician working alone.

Sailors counted the knots on the rope
as the sand ran through the hour-glass.

What is speed?

Speed is the relationship between a distance and the time taken to cover it. Often it is calculated using the distance you can cover in an hour; a car, for instance, may be said to travel at 50 k.p.h. (50 kilometres per hour). Some aeroplanes can travel even faster than sound. The speed of sound is called Mach (about 1,220 k.p.h.) and the speed of aircraft is measured in the number of Mach they travel. The speed at which a boat moves is measured in knots, because sailors used to work out their speed by using a rope which had knots tied in it at regular intervals. They let the rope out behind the boat, measuring the time with an hour-glass. The more knots that were paid out into the water, the faster the boat was travelling.

Measuring how hard the wind is blowing

Wind-speed is measured by using an anemometer. Admiral Beaufort worked out a scale for wind-speeds.

In some sports you need to measure time to a hundredth of a second, so you use a chronometer.

Measuring the Earth

As the Earth rotates on its axis, different countries receive the sun's light one after another. When the sun rises in Europe, it is night in America and midday in India. Scientists divide the world into time-zones by drawing imaginary lines around the Earth. These lines are the meridians, which were used to calculate the metre.

1. Meridians   2. The Equator

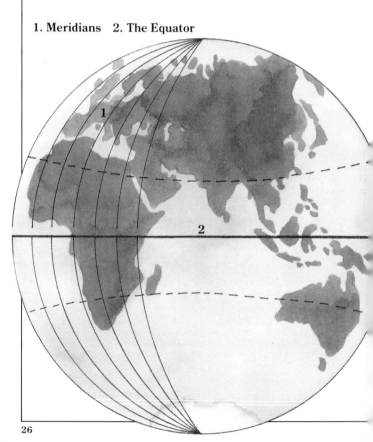

The nocturlabe, like the astrolabe, is an old-fashioned instrument which tells the time by measuring the height of the stars above the horizon.

The most famous meridian of all passes through London and is called the Greenwich Meridian. When sailors need to work out where they are at sea, they calculate their position east or west of the Greenwich Meridian and north or south of the Equator. This is another imaginary line circling the Earth half-way between the two Poles.

By using a sextant to measure the angle between the sun and the horizon, the navigator can work out the boat's position at sea.

It is hot and sunny. The temperature and the air pressure are high.

It is hot, but stormy. The temperature is high, but the pressure is low.

It is cold and fine. The pressure is high, but the temperature is low.

Sunshine and rain

Measuring heat, cold and humidity, forecasting changes in weather – all these are the tasks of meteorologists.

Barometer

Thermometers measure heat.

Celsius and Fahrenheit each invented a system of measuring temperature. The centigrade or Celsius system takes the freezing point of water as 0°C, and the boiling point of water as 100°C, whereas in the Fahrenheit system water freezes at 32°F and boils at 212°F. Thermometers show the temperature by means of mercury or alcohol which expand or contract inside a glass tube as it gets hotter or colder. **Barometers** show changes in air pressure. The weather is very much affected by air pressure, which is measured in millibars. The needle on the barometer moves as the pressure changes.

Clinical thermometer for measuring a person's temperature

Weather thermometer

Measuring electricity

There are a lot of different ways of measuring electricity, all named after the people who first discovered them. Volts are named after an Italian scientist, Volta, who invented the electric battery. The more electricity a battery produces, the higher the voltage. Amps are named after the French scientist, Ampère,

who measured the number of
electrons travelling along a wire
charged with electricity. The wattage
of a light-bulb or of an appliance
refers to the amount of power that it
uses. Most domestic light-bulbs are
between 60 and 100 watts, while a vacuum-
cleaner may be 1,000 watts. Watts are
named after James Watt, a Scottish
scientist.

By counting the number of seconds between the flash of lightning and the sound of thunder, you can work out how far away the thunder-storm is.

Why do you see lightning *before* you hear the crack of thunder during a storm? Because **light travels faster than sound**. In one second, sound only travels 360m, whereas light travels 300,000 km. The speed of light is the fastest known speed in the universe.

Because they know the speed at which light travels, scientists are able to work out the vast distances between the stars. These distances are calculated in light-years, that is, the distance travelled by light in a year, which is about ten thousand billion kilometres! A laser beam can reach the moon in one and a quarter seconds, and get to Mars in twenty minutes.

Measuring the tiniest sizes

Viruses are the smallest organisms in the world; they measure only a few millionths of a millimetre, but they are still much bigger than atoms. The smallest known atom is the hydrogen atom, which measures one half-angstrom – one millimetre divided by 20 million!

Using a telescope to observe the stars

Measuring shapes

Geometry is the science of measuring shapes. Here are three geometrical shapes which you can make for yourself out of stiff paper.

A cone: flat on the table, the shape for a cone can be a quarter of a circle. When you join the straight sides together, you get a cone shape with a circle for the base.

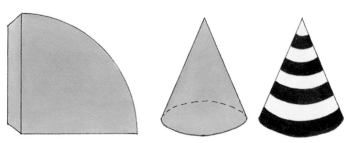

Copy this pattern, as small or as big as you like, on to stiff paper. Cut it out and stick the flap to the straight side with glue.

You can make your cone into a hat or a face or a little creature.

A cube: to make a cube, you need to use a ruler to measure the sides very carefully and make sure they are all the same length.

If you score along the lines before you fold them, you will get a neater shape.

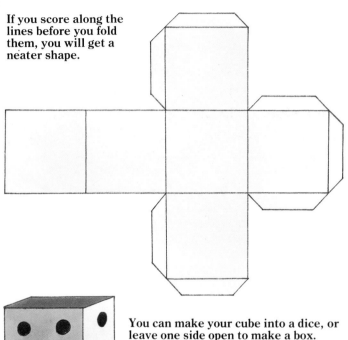

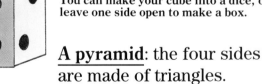

You can make your cube into a dice, or leave one side open to make a box.

A pyramid: the four sides are made of triangles.

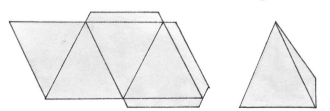

Index

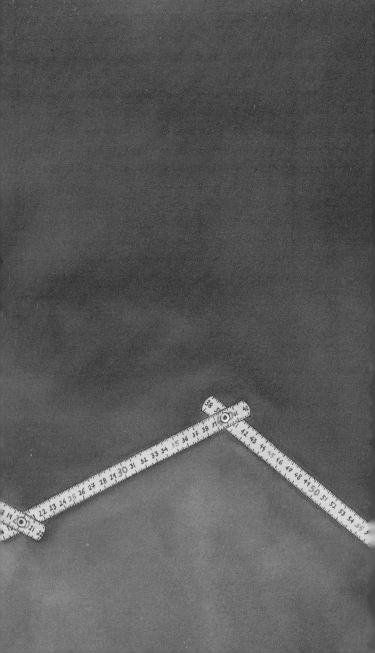